WISDOM
FROM
ABOVE

WISDOM
FROM
ABOVE

450 Quotes

By Kornah Flowers

ARPress
45 Dan Road Suite 5
Canton MA 02021
Hotline: 1(888) 821-0229
Fax: 1(508) 545-7580

Ordering Information:
Quantity sales. Special discounts are available on quantity purchases by corporations, associations, and others. For details, contact the publisher at the address above.

Printed in the United States of America.

ISBN-13:   Softcover   979-8-89676-240-9
                   eBook   979-8-89676-241-6

Library of Congress Control Number: 2024927260

Dedicated To:

My Closest And Most Meaningful Friend,
The Precious Holy Spirit,
Who Thought It Not Robbery To Speak The Wisdom
God Spoke To Me And Through Me So Often.
Thank You, Precious Holy Spirit,
You Are My Best Friend Forever.

Introduction

Proverbs 25:11

A Word Fitly Spoken Is Like Apples Of Gold
In Pictures Of Silver.

The More Excuses You Give Yourself,
The Less You Become Your Best.

—◆—

Excuses Do Not Make Your Life Better;
They Make Your Life Stagnant.

—◆—

Excuses Do Not Bring Back The Blessings You
Missed Because You Did Not Do What Was Required,
When It Was Required, How It Was Required,
And With Whom It Was Required.

Man's Greatest Problem Is EXCUSES
And Man's Best Solution Is SELF- DISCIPLINE.

—m—

Excuses Got Fired, He Doesn't Work For Anybody
Anymore. His Service Is No Longer Needed In
Your Lifetime. His License To Operate Is Expired,
Revoked By God, And Banned By The Government
Of Best Life.

—m—

Excuses Was Replaced By Mr. Diligence
And Positive-Attitude A Long Time Ago.

The Only Thing Standing Between You
And Greatness Are Your Excuses.
Get Rid Of Excuses And Enter Your Greatness.

—⁓—

Stop Giving Excuses.

—⁓—

Your Laziness And Excuses Can Slow Down
Or Hinder What God Wants To Get Done
On Time, In And Through You.

Procrastination Kills Purpose Because
Everything Is For A Time And A Reason.

—◆—

Procrastination Will Cause You To Live
An Unfulfilled Life.

—◆—

Procrastination Will Keep You Struggling
And Determination Will Keep You Winning.

Time Is The Highest Commodity On The Market.
It Cannot Be Replaced.

—ᴡ—

Time Is The Keeper Of Everyone's Lifespan.

—ᴡ—

Don't Relax Or Else You Will Lose.
Keep Moving Forward Faster.
Time Waits For No One.

Time And Choice Combined Is The Door
To Everything And Everyone.

—m—

Every Blessing, Every Business And Every
Opportunity Has An Opening And Closing Hours.
That Is Why Seeing Your Point Of Entry And
Entering On Time Is Very Important.

—m—

Every Building And Every Blessing Has An Entry Point.
That Entry Point Could Be In The Form Of A Door,
A Connection Or Conversation With Someone, A Position,
A Gift, Talent Or Skill, An Action Or Reaction, A Decision,
A Relocation, An Act Of Kindness Or Even A Place,
Relationship, Etc. But If You Are Spiritually Blind To Your
Entry Point Or Door Into Your Blessings And The Timing,
You Will Remain Stagnant And Begging.

Great Accomplishments Demand
Timely Right Actions.

—⁂—

Solution Is In Timely Action.

—⁂—

The Only Time You Have Is Now.
Put The Talent, Gift Or Skill To Work Now That
God Has Given You And Make The Most Of It.
Every Moment Is Your Now Moment.

When You Do The Right Things At The Right Times,
They Produce Wonderful Results.

—◊—

Every Living Human Being Rich Or Poor,
Big Or Small, Educated Or Uneducated Regardless
Of Your Geographical Location Or Status In Life,
Have Direct Access To Twenty-Four Hours Every Day.
Everyone Has Equal Amount Of Time Every Day.
You Can Choose To Invest Your Time In The Right
Things To Produce Quality Results Or You Can Waste
Your Precious Time Behind Things And People That
Will Keep Your Life Stagnant. Where You Invest Your
Time, Is Where You Will See Results.

—◊—

Timing Is Everything.
Timing Determines The Value Of A Thing
And The Impact Of Its Results To The User.

No Eagle Flies With Another Eagle Wings.
Take Full Responsibility For The Results You Desire.
Find The Right Way, And Get It Done On Time.

If A Person Or Thing Cannot Fulfill Their Reason
For Existence In Their Time, They Become Irrelevant,
Useless, Unfulfilled And Miserable.

Nothing Is Useful Unless
It Is Finished Well On Time.

Even The Right Decision Made Too Late
Is Of No Effect.

—⁓—

The More Late You Are In Doing A Thing,
The Less Valuable It Becomes And The Lesser Impact
It Has. Late Comers Are Always Embarrassed.

—⁓—

Lateness Prevents The Fulfillment Of Purpose
And Causes You To Pay More For Less.

Lateness Restrain Your Potentials. Lateness Makes Others Question Your Ability To Handle Leadership Responsibilities. Lateness Takes Away From Your Personalities. Lateness Denies You Entry. Lateness Is A Prime Thief Of Your Resources. Every Time You Are Late Paying A Bill They Charge You More.

—⁓—

Lateness Is A Thief Of Your Integrity And Resources. How Late Are You For Your Prayer Time Or Devotional Time With God? How Late Are You For Appointments With Man? How Late Are You For Work Every Week? How Late Are You When Making Payments? How Late Are You In Keeping Your Promises? Lateness Is One Of Your Major Enemies, Not Your Friend.

—⁓—

Stop Being Late For Everything.

Doing Things Early Delivers You From Last Minute
Stress, Poor Performance And Unnecessary Mistakes.

—m—

Doing Things Early Automatically Puts You Ahead
In The Game Of Life And Gives You Advantages
Over Your Competitors.

—m—

Rising Up Early Is A Godly Requirement
For Great Accomplishments.

Your Shining Is Hidden In Your Rising.
If You Don't Rise Up, You Will Never Shine.
Your Gift Will Only Make Room For You
If You Develop It.

—m—

There Will Be No Perfect Time.
If It Is Not Raining, It's Going To Be Snowing.
If It Is Not Snowing, The Sun Will Be Shinning Very Hot.
You Are Getting Older And Your Energy Is Measure.
There Will Come A Time You Will Not Be Able To Do
What You Can Do Now. That Is Why You Need To
Rise Up And Do It Now.

—m—

Don't Let The Reason For Your Existence Be
Unfulfilled Why Your Time Swiftly Passes You By.
Wake Up And Go To Work. Now Is Your Time.

Wake Up Every Morning Running With Your Divine
Plan For The Day Because Time Is The Fastest Jet
That Waits For No One.

—⚬—

Waking Up Every Morning Energized Is The Greatest
Blessing Anyone Can Have. If You Were A Billionaire And
You Do Not Wake Up, That's The End Of Your Show.
If You Were The Most Educated, Most Talented,
Most Beautiful And Most Handsome And You Do Not
Wake Up, That Is The End Of Your Show.

—⚬—

There Is No Time Without Life
And There Is No Life Without Time.

Life Is Not As Long As It Looks. Life Is So Brief.
Divert Or Invest Your Time, Energy And Resources In
The Right Things, Right People, Right Jobs And Right
Places. Your Returns Will Be Beneficial And Rewarding.
Only What We Do For Christ Is Eternal.
Everything You Have Is Measured And Limited.
Be Mindful Of Who And What You Invest It In.

—◊—

Live Like Your Life Is On A Temporary Timer
Because It Is.

—◊—

Arrival Leads To Departure.
When You Arrive, You Depart.

Only A Moment Of Life And Time Have Been
Assigned To Each One By God To Fulfill His
Purpose On The Earth. Don't Waste Your Moment.

—m—

Your Life Is Like A Flashing Vapor.
Now Is The Only Time You Have.
The Next Minute Could Be Your Last Minute.
Don't Waste Your Time.

—m—

Every Day That Goes By,
Is One Day Deducted From All Of Our Lives.
You Don't Have Time To Fool Around.

Life Doesn't Care About Where You Came
From Or What You Are Going Through.
Life Cares About What Positive Difference You
Are Making Each Day Right Where You Are.

Get Back Up Now. Run Faster Now.
Get It Done Now. Humble Yourself Now.
Forgive Others And Make Up Now.
Make Time For Your Family Now.

Time Is The Most Valuable Thing In This World.
What Good Is Lots Of Money If You Have No Time To
Spend It. What Good Are Material Things If You Have
No Time Enjoy Them With Your Love Ones.

Things Can Never Replace Time.
Time With Your Family Is One Of The Most Valuable
Things In This World. The Things You Teach And Learn,
The Fun You Share, The Places You Go And The Things
You Do Together Have A Greater Positive Impact Than
Any Amount Of Money Or Costly Things.
Time Is Priceless.

—◦◦◦—

Everything And Everyone Is For A Time And A Reason.
Make The Most Of Your Time And Fulfill The Reason
For Your Connection.

—◦◦◦—

You Can Only Make The Most Of Your Time When
You Understand The Purpose Of The Time You Are In.

Those Who Do Not Remain In The Lord
Always Expire Before Their Time.

23

—ɷ—

Timely Attention Is The Difference Between
Life And Death, Success And Failure.

—ɷ—

Many People Do Not Die For The Lack Of Medical
Expertise, Advance Equipment And Effective Medicine.
They Die For The Lack Of Timely Attention.

When You Don't Know Where You're Going
In Life, Everywhere Becomes Important.

———m———

When You Know Whose You Are, Who You Are,
What You Have, And Where You Are Heading;
You Don't Follow The Crowd Instead You Be Yourself.

———m———

When You Don't Discover Who You Are,
You Want To Be Like Everybody Else,
And You Won't Know Where To Succeed.

The Story Is Never True
From The Outside View.

—⚋—

The Way You Carry Yourself Reflects
On Everybody You Represent,
So Carry Yourself Well.

—⚋—

Image Is The Viewers Interpretation
Of Yourself Presentation.

The Crowd Is Not Always Right.

—m—

People Who Make A Difference,
Don't Make Noise.

—m—

You've Got To Be Different To Make A Difference.
The Difference Is What Matters. The Difference Stands Out.
The Difference Attracts Attention And Gain Support
So Find Pleasure In Being Different In A Positive Way.

You Can Only Make A Difference
By Being Different.

27

—m—

Everyone Falls Occasionally But Wise,
And Great People Rise Up Quickly
And Do Things Different.

—m—

Change Is The Controller
Of Everyone's Lifestyle.

You Will Have To Change. Change Is The Essence Of Life. Anything Or Anyone Who Is Not Changing Is Not Growing. Anything That Is Not Growing Is Slowly Dying. In Life We Change From Babies To Teens, From Teens To Young Adults, From Young Adults To Adults, From Adults To Elders And From Elders To Aged. Making Good Changes Always Reveals The Better You.

—m—

Every Change For The Better In A Believer's Life, Start With A New Heart Which Comes From God By Faith, And A New Mindset Which Comes From Replacing Your Old Mindset With His Word.

—m—

In Order To Stay Relevant, You Must Keep Changing For The Better.

When You Don't Listen To God's Warning
Privately And Change Your Ways,
You Will Embarrass Yourself Publicly.

—m—

It Only Takes One Decision To Change Our Position
In Life From Worse To Better Or From Better To Worse.

—m—

Sometimes, It Is Not What Happened To Us In Life
That Changes Our Lives For The Better Or Worse
But What We Make Of What Happened.

If You Do Not Control Your Body,
It Will Make You Lose The Prize Awaiting You.

—⁕—

When You Yield To Your Flesh,
You Will Settle For Less And Forfeit The Best.

—⁕—

Let Your Inner Decision
Control Your Outward Behavior.

Self-Discipline Is The Engine
Behind Great Accomplishments.

31

—m—

Winning Any Race Requires Self-Discipline.

—m—

Without Self-Discipline, We Become A Problem
To Ourselves And Useless To Others.

Only Those Who Dare To Try Harder Again,
Can Break The Borders Of False Limitations Placed
On Their Lives By The Wrong Mindset.

—⟋⟍—

Failure Is Refusing To Get Back Up
Whenever You Fall And Do Things Differently.

—⟋⟍—

As You Climb Up To Great Places,
Be Careful Of How You Climb And What
And Who You Use As The Ladder.

Don't Step On Others To Get To The Top
But Build On What Others Have Done To Reach Higher
And Achieve More Than They Could Have Achieve.

—⚊—

Hardship Is The Foundation Of Greatness.
The Solidness Of Your Foundation Determines
The Height Of Your Greatness.

—⚊—

Greatness Is Never Produced
From A Comfortable Place.

Comfort Is The Pathway
To Limitations.

—m—

Inconvenience Is The Pathway
To Greatness.

—m—

The Pressure Of The Earth On Top
Of The Seed Is Necessary For The Growth
Of The Seed And Germination Of The Seed.
You Are The Seed Of Abraham.

One Of The Major Enemies To Your
Next Level Of Success Is Convenience.

35

—⁓—

Sometimes, Convenience Can Rob Us
Of Achieving A Greater Destiny.

—⁓—

Be Consistent And Precise,
You Will Achieve Great Things.

Consistency Is The Thread That Sews
The Pieces Together To Make Something Whole,
Useful And Beautiful.

—⚏—

Being Consistent And Persistent
Will Make You Finish Well On Time.

—⚏—

Consistency Is An Effect That Makes A Person
Productive In Any Area Of Their Life.

If You Stay At It, You Will Succeed At It.
Being Consistent Brings Out The Greatness In You.
Being Consistent Brings Mastery To Your Gifts And Skills.

Only Those Who Start Can Continue,
And Only Those Who Continue Can Finish
Well On Time And Win.

There Are More Good Reasons Why You Need To
Rise Up And Become Consistently Committed To Your
Goals Than There Are Reasons Why You Cannot Do It.

We Become What We Consistently
Think, Believe, Say And Do.

—m—

Too Many Breaks Sometimes Break Things Up.
Stay Focus And Be Consistent.

—m—

Too Much Physical Rest Is For The Dead.
It Is Usually Said "May Your Soul Rest In Peace"
When You Are Dead.

Too Much Loud Physical Noise Is A Nuisance
To Your Soul, Cut It Off. It Is In Divine Quietness
We Find Wisdom, Strength, Peace, And Direction.

There Are Only Two Options In Life.
They Are Excuses Or Winning Results And Rewards.
No Matter How Justifiable Or Pitiful Our Excuses Are;
They Are Still Excuses. "Oh Because" Doesn't Change Our
Results. Wake Up, Do Something Different On Time.

The Test Of Strength Is Determined By The Weight We
Carry, The Battles We Fight, And The Victories We Win,
The Temptations We Overcome, And The Struggles We
Survived. Stay Determined.

Determination Makes Great Men And Women.
Determination Will Always Overcome Situations
No Matter How Difficult They Are.

—m—

I Cannot Live By My Feelings Because I Have
Genuine Reasons To Press Harder And Do Better.

—m—

Runners Are Winners And Winners Are Runners
You Must Become Faster And More Accurate
In Your Work.

We Are The Sum Of Our Thoughts
And The Multiplication Of Our Actions.

—m—

Life Will Always Serve You Consequences Or
Blessings Based Upon Your Choices And Actions.

—m—

Remember, You Control Your Choices No
Matter How Strong The Outside Influence Is.
You Will Have To Deal With The Results So
Always Follow Your Heart And Make The Right
And Wise Choice.

Life Is About Perceptions, Decisions,
Accepting Responsibilities, And Actions.

42

———∞———

Nothing Is Achieved Without Sacrifice.

———∞———

Sacrifice Brings Rest To Issues.

Life Is Like A Stage Of Actors.
You Get On At Birth And You Get Off At Death.
What Matters Most Is Not The Length Of Time
You Spend On The Stage But How Well You Perform
And What You Accomplish While On The Stage.

—m—

Things Come With Time, Hard Work And Stage.
Wait For Your Time And Stage. When You Get
On The Stage Before Your Time, You Will Get Off
The Stage Before Your Time.

—m—

Some Folks Never Enjoy Any Stage In Their Lives
Because They Are Never Satisfied. Learn To Enjoy
Where You Are, Each Stage Along The Way Because
Things Change Quicker Than You Expect.

Life Is About Purpose, Not Pleasure.
Nothing Is Evaluated, Validated Or Appreciated
Based Upon Its Pleasure But Based Upon The
Fulfillment Of Its Purpose.

—m—

Be Purpose Driven And Not Strongly Attached To
Anything.

—m—

Your True Value In This World Depends On Your
Fulfillment Of Your God Given Purpose.

Life Is About The Fulfillment Of Purpose.

45

—m—

You Will Never Find Your Purpose In Things
But You Can Always Accumulate Things
As You Fulfill Your Purpose In Life.

—m—

You Will Never Discover Your Purpose
Until You Come To Your Creator—God,
Because The Purpose Of A Product Is
Determined Before It Made.

Our Purpose Keeps Us Learning, Growing,
Moving, And Fulfilling; Whereas Being Strongly
Attached To Things, Places, And People Keep
Us Stuck, Frustrated And Unfulfilled.

—◊—

A Product Does Not Give Value To Its Purpose
But The Purpose Gives Value To The Product.

—◊—

Requirement Is The Ingredient For The Deployment
Of Any Precise Personality, Or The Making Of
Any Precise Product To Fulfill A Specific Purpose.

When We Ignore The Importance Of Requirements,
We Forfeit The Benefits Of Why They Were Required.

47

If You Don't Follow God's Direction,
You Will Never Get To Your Divine Destination.

God Can Make An Ugly Situation Become
Your Transportation To A Great Destination.

It Is Not The Smoothness Or Roughness
Of The Road You Are On That Matters.
What Matters Most; Is The Road Taking
You To Your Divine Destination.

—m—

When Your Head In The Wrong Direction,
You Will Always Have Incidents, Accidents
And Long Delays To Fulfilling Your Purpose
And Reaching Your Divine Destination.

—m—

No Matter Where You Are Going
Or What You Desire To Accomplish,
You Must Head In The Right Direction
In Order To Arrive At Your Desired
Destination On Time.

Don't Let Your Condition Become Your Justification
For Not Getting To Your Divine Destination.

—m—

Believe That Your Condition Is Never Your Conclusion
But An Aspiration For Your Transformation To A Better
Destination.

—m—

Sometimes Your Most Hurtful Moments,
Can Become Your Most Transforming
Moments Into Your Glorious Destination.
God Can Use The Hurts From Your Hurters
To Enable You To Develop Eagle Wings
To Soar To Heights Unknown.

You Look Like You Are Behind Because
God Is Using Your Delay To Keep You Working
Toward On A Better Destination.

—m—

Prayer Is Your Connection With Heaven
For Direction To Your Destination.

—m—

Rejection By Man Is Direction From God
To A Glorious Destination.

Rejection By Man Can Become
Direction From God.

—〰—

God Can Reverse Your Disappointment
With Man Into A Life Changing Appointment
With Him.

—〰—

The Worst From Man Always Leads
To The Best From God.

Good Reminders Keep Us Moving In The Right
Direction Because So Often We Tend
To Quickly Forget Important Lessons, People,
And Places That We Ought To Remember The Most.

—⁂—

When You Look In God's Direction,
You Will See Your Blessings Flowing.
When You Stay In God's Direction,
You Will Keep Your Blessings Flowing.
In God's Direction You Will Find
His Provision And Protection.

—⁂—

You Will Always Discover God's Supernatural
Provision, When You Arrived On Time At
The Place God Tells You To Go.

When God Speaks To You To Do Something,
He Has Already Spoken In Advance To Everything
And Everybody Else Needed To Make What He
Told You Become A Reality. As You Obey God Fully,
You Will Discover His Unlimited, Awaiting, Hidden
Resources Needed For Every Stage Of The
Process Of Fulfillment.

———✺———

God Can Do Anything, Anytime And Anywhere.
He Is All Powerful. God Does Not Need Permission
From Anyone To Bless Your Life And Change
How Your Story Ends.

———✺———

God Can Do Something For You And Through
You That He Has Done For No One Else.

God's Power Is Available To Everyone
Who Believes In Him So That They Can
See The Impossible Become Possible And
The Invisible Become Visible.

—m—

God Only Receives, Blesses, Multiplies And
Make Better That Which Is Placed In His Hands.
Place Every Aspect Of Your Life In God's Hands.

—m—

When You Want Something From God,
You Must Stay Focus. Avoid Distractions And
Fleshly Gratification As Much As Possible.
They Are Your Two Major Enemies That Will
Mislead To Your Disqualification.

Distractions And Fleshly Gratification
Equal Disqualification.

Everything About God Is Based Upon Two Words.
That Word Is Trust And Obedience.

Your Level Of Trust In God Determines What You
Will Receive From Him And God's Level Of Trust
In You Based Upon Your Faithfulness With Little
In Public And Private Determines What God Will
Continue To Release To You. Can God Trust You
To Do Things His Way?

When God Or Someone Trust You With Their Stuff,
You Are Expected And Required To Do Things Their
Way Not Yours. The Easier Way To Lose Access To
Many Blessings Is To Keep Betraying The Trust Placed
In You And Keep Giving Excuses For Not Doing
What Is Expected Or Required.

—⁂—

Trust Is The Greatest Award
Anyone Can Achieve.

—⁂—

Trust Opens Unending Doors. Trust Give You
Access To The Wealth Of Others. Trust Puts You
In Charge When You Ought Not To Be In Charge.
Trust Causes People To Be At Ease Around You.
Trust Makes Your Word Valuable To Others.
Trust Will Cause You To Be Highly Recommended.
Trust Will Attract Unending Customers To The
Service You Provide.

Trust Is Not Earned By What You Say Repeatedly
But What You Do Consistently.

—⚍—

Trust Demands Being Honest And Treating
Others Fairly Whether You Like Them
Or The Way They Treat You.

—⚍—

Stuff Is A Byproduct Of Trust.
God And Man Will Give You Stuff Once
You Can Prove Yourself Trustworthy.

Your Belief Is Your Password
To Access Your Inheritance In Christ.

—m—

Never Based Your Belief In God Upon What
Makes Sense Or What You See With Your Natural
Eyes. God Supersedes All Of That. He Is Invisible And All
Powerful. God Can Do Anything, Anywhere And Anytime.

—m—

Everything That You See With Your Eyes Was Made
From What You Don't See, That Includes You And Me.
Once We Were Not In Existence Physically And Now We
Are In Existence. The Invisible Is The Producer Of The
Visible. When You Want Something To Be Made Visible,
Look To Him Who Is Invisible And He Will Give You
Wisdom And Direction As To How To Make It Visible.

Doubt Is An Evil Spirit That Keeps You Stuck
In Your Worst, And Rob You Of Your Best.

———

Doubt Is A Thief Of Your Prepaid Blessings.

———

Don't Wait Too Late To Believe
And Act Upon God's Word.

The Purpose Of Faith Is Not Get Stuff From God
But To Develop Trust In God.

—◊—

The Place Of Trust Is The Place Of Faith.
The Place Of Faith Is The Place Of God's Pleasure.
The Place Of God's Pleasure Is The Place Of God's Powers.
The Place Of God's Power Is The Place Of Unlimited
Miracles.

—◊—

Until Faith Is Released,
Blessings Are Not Disbursed.

Faith Requires Faithfulness With What God Has Trusted You With For There To Be A Continuous Fruitfulness. You Cannot Be Fruitful God's Way If You Are Not Faithful. Prayer Is Like An Expressed Lane And Faith Is Like A U-Haul Truck That Get Your Stuff From The Invisible Realm To The Visible Realm.

Faith Comes By Hearing Jesus
Who Is The Living Word Of God.
Results Come By Obeying Jesus
Who Is The Fulfilled Word Of God.

Your Obedience Is God's Ingredient
For Your Miracles.

Obey His God's Voice And Word Now,
So That Your End Results Are Amazing
And Not Regrets.

—ⱮⱮ—

Your Protection Is Always In Your Decisions
And Your Blessings Are Always In Your
Obedience To God.

—ⱮⱮ—

Your Obedience To God Is Your Spiritual
Phone Call To Every Blessing God Has In
Store For You.

When You Walk By Faith,
You Will Go Through A Process Of Self-Denial
But You Will Not Be Disappointed At The End.

—m—

The Consequences Of Not Walking By Faith
Is To Lose All The Great Things God Wants To Do
In You, Through You And For You.

—m—

Walk By Faith And Gain
Or Walk By Sight And Lose.

Nothing Is Done Right, Unless It Is Done
From The Right Spirit And With The Right Spirit.

It Is Spirit That Impacts Spirit. Our Service To God
And Others Is Never Blessed Until Our Spirit Is Right.
God Looks At Our Hearts, Not Our Outward Appearance
And Performance. He Knows The View From The
Outside Is Never True Because The Truth Is Within.

—◊—

The Holy Spirit Is Your Divine Helper.
Ask Him To Help You.

—◊—

Do Not Wait Until You Fail Or Lose
Before You Choose To Obey The Voice Of The
Holy Spirit. His Guidance Will Make Your
Results Amazing And Instead Of Regrettable.

The Residues Of God's Presence Are Your Equipment
For Your Next Victory Over Any And Every Situation
So Spend Quality Time In God's Presence.

—◊—

God Is With You Every Step Of The
Way To Help You.

—◊—

Your Situation Is A Distraction To Prevent You
From Looking Up To God For The Help You Need.
God Helps Everyone Who Looks To Him And
Obey His Strategy.

Other Than The Holy Spirit,
Some Of The Greatest Influences In This World
Is Love And Kindness, Lack And Pain.

———

Only The Holy Spirit Knows Your Blessings
Manifestation Timing. Therefore, Obey Divine
Signals With A Sense Of Urgency So You Can
Step Into The Arrangements Made By Heaven
On Your Behalf.

———

GPS Is Only Useful To Moving Things And People.
Spirit Led Movement Is Proof That You Are
Alive In Christ.

Light Is A Divine Voice That Shows
What To Do And Where To Go.
Stay With The Light And In The Light.

—⟋⟍—

You Can Only Go Or Progress In The Direction You
Are Looking And Seeing. When You Look Or See Up,
You Put Your Mind In An Upward Thinking Position,
You Climb And Go Up. When You Look Or See Down,
You Put Your Mind In A Downward Thinking Position.
You Stumble And Fall Down. When You Look Forward,
You Put Your Mind In A Forward Thinking Position Or
Motion. You Walk, Run Or Drive Or Leap Forward.
When You Look Backwards, You Put Your Mind In A
Backward Thinking Motion Or Position. You Reverse,
You Regress, You Go Backwards And Sometimes You
Have Major Accidents Because The Light Is Green At
This Moment Indicating That You Go Forward.

—⟋⟍—

Sheep Does Not Lead And Protect The Shepherd.
It Is The Shepherd Who Leads And Protects The Sheep
Because The Shepherd Knows More Than The Sheep.
Wild Animals Are Not Afraid Of The Sheep, But They
Are Afraid Of The Shepherd. Follow The Leading
Of The Shepherd And Stay With The Sheepfold,
You Will Be Fed And Kept Safe.

The Closer You Draw Toward God The Clearer
You See Because He Is The Perfect Light And He Is
The Way To All Genuine Fulfillment Of Purpose,
Success And Prosperity. The Higher You Press Toward
God And His Things, The Further You See Because
He Is The Highest Of The Highest. He Is Above All.

—⁂—

The Enlightening Of Your Eyes Of Understanding
Will Break The Circle Of Limitations Over Every
Aspect Of Your Life And Ministry.

—⁂—

Only When The Eyes Of Your Understanding
Are Lifted Up Above Your Situation, The King Of Glory
Comes In With Strength, Deliverance And Victory.

The Eyes Of Your Understanding See The Creation
And Completion Of Things In The Invisible Realm
Long Before They Are Accomplished In The Physical
World. All Things Are Created And Accomplished Twice,
First In The Mind Then In The Physical By Our Plans
And Timely Action.

—⟪—

Until You Lift Up The Eyes Of Your Understanding,
You Will Not See The Invisible Glorious Place God
Is Taking You. Stop Looking Down On Yourself And
Allowing Your Condition To Become Your Conclusion
And Your History To Control Your Mindset
And Daily Conversation.

—⟪—

The Real Things That Are Yet To Come,
Are Never Seen With The Physical Eyes First
But With The Eyes Of Our Understanding.

Spiritual Blindness Is The Worst Condition
Any Believer Can Be In.

—m—

You Can Never Give The Right Answers To
A Question Or A Positive Solution To A Problem
When You Perceive Things Wrongly.

—m—

Seeing With The Mind Of Your Understanding,
Is Knowing That You Have, What You Have Seen.

Understanding Is The Secret Of How Things Work.

71

—m—

Understanding Is Our Freedom From Struggling.
What We Don't Understand, We Stand Under Struggling
Instead Of Standing On Top With Great Success.

—m—

It Is Our Understanding That Makes Us
Outstanding When We Apply The Wisdom Of God.

Seek God For Wisdom And Understanding.
They Are Necessities For Successful Living.

—m—

Get Understanding By Learning From Those
Who Have Produced Amazing Results.

—m—

The Understanding And Application
Of Right Knowledge Are The Difference
Between Success And Failure.

Every Struggle Is A Product Of Lack Of Knowledge,
And Every Success Is A Product Of The Right Knowledge
Gained, Understood And Applied At The Right Time.

—◊◊◊—

Two Key Things That Make Us Valuable Are
Advance Relevant Knowledge And Mastery Skills.

—◊◊◊—

The World Will Keep Paying You For What
You Know And Keep Producing In A Better Form.

Study To Display That You Have Improved First
Spiritually, Second, Mentally And In Every Aspect
Of Your Life So That You Can Be Approved In
Every Aspect Of Your Life.

—m—

You Cannot Improve
And Be Approved Without Studying.

—m—

Nothing Is Good Unless God Approves It.

Don't Let The Pain Of The Cross Cause You
To Divert From The Purpose Of Your Cross.

—⁓—

The Cross Is Painful But The Rewards Are Plentiful,
Glorious, Amazing, Fulfilling, Satisfying, Permanent,
Generational Etc.

—⁓—

The Pain And Shame Of The Cross
Don't Last But The Abundance Of Blessings,
And High Position Last Forever.

Endure Your Cross Whatever Form It Takes
Because Of Your Mission.

—m—

Endure With The Right Attitude, It Will Soon Be Over,
And You Will Be Seated In A Position Of Great Rewards,
Great Results, And Great Power.

—m—

Endure Your Cross Whatever Form It Takes.
Your Mission Is To Fulfill God's Purpose.
God Is Your Rewarder.

It's Not The Cross That Really Matters
But The Purpose You Accomplish
While On Your Cross.

—◊◊◊—

One Of The Purposes Of Your Situational Cross
Is To Kill Your Character Weaknesses, And Give
More Life And Power To Your Strengths.

—◊◊◊—

Your Situational Cross, Attitude,
And Words Have A Life Changing Effect
On Your Haters And Your Lovers.

In Public Or Private, Let Your Thoughts,
Your Words, And Your Deeds Reflect Christ
While You Are On Your Situational Cross.

In Public Or Private, Let Your Thoughts,
Your Words And Your Deeds Reflect Christ
By Growing In The World.

When God's Purpose Is Fulfilled,
He Rewards You And Others.

All Trees Do Not Bear Fruits At The Same Time.
Your Season Is Coming And Your Fruits Will Be
Better And Bigger.

—⟶⟵—

Nothing And No One Grow
Without Patience.

—⟶⟵—

Everything Takes Time To Grow.
Anything That Grows Overnight,
Ends Up Dying Overnight.
Any Fruit That Gets Ripe Soon,
Gets Rotten Soon, Gets Forgotten Soon.

Take Time To Grow Up Young People.
Enjoy Your Youth, It Is Precious.
If You Do All That Adults Do While You
Are A Youth, What Will Be Left For You
To Do When You Become An Adult.

—w—

Boys In Men Bodies And Girls In Women Bodies.
The Development Of Your Body Does Not Depicts
The Maturity Of Your Mind. You Can Have A Fully
Developed Body And A Very, Very Immature Mind
And Spirit Which Makes You Vulnerable.

—w—

It Is The Engine And Functions That Determine
The Durability Of A Car And The Price Of Its Value,
Not The Paint Or Tint On The Outside So, Also The
True Value Of A Man Or Woman Is In Their Character,
And Not Their Looks.

Good Looks And Things Do Not
Determine Someone's Character.

—◊◊◊—

It Does Not Matter How Beautiful Or How Handsome
Your Face Looks Or How Well Defined Your Body
Structure Is, If Your Ways Are Ugly And Your Character
Is Bad, You Are A Very Ugly Person Because Your
Ways Affect People Far Greater Than Your Looks.

—◊◊◊—

Good Ways/Habits Have A Greater Impact
Than Good Looks.

Young Girls Of Today, Become Great Women
Of Tomorrow By Choosing Books And Personal
Development First Over Boys And Babies.

—m—

It Is Wise To Take Time Just To Become
Good Friends Before You Become Lovers.
Time And Observance Will Teach You A Lot
About People Without You Paying A Penny.

—m—

Too Many People Are Hurt In Relationship
Or Stuck With Their Nightmare All Because
They Chose To Ignore The Red Flags In The
Character Of The Other Person.

No One Is Perfect, But You Deserve
Someone Suitable.

Nothing Multiplies Without Women.
God Bless Them And Said Be Fruitful And Multiply,
But Mankind Cannot Multiply Without Women.

—m—

Nothing Is Complete Without Women.
God Said It Is Not Good For A Man To Be Alone.
A Man's Completion And Satisfaction Are Hidden
In A Suitable Female Helper Called A Biological Wife.

—m—

Can God Make Mistakes? No.
God Only Blesses What God Accepts.
God Only Accepts What God Prescribes.
God Prescribed Marriage To Consist Of A
Union Between One Man And One Woman.

Never Give Your Self To Someone Who
Does Not Know Your Value And Purpose.
They Will Treat You Like Trash.
They Will Use You And Misuse You.

—⁂—

Never Be Excited To Meet With Nobody
More Than You Are To Meet With God.

—⁂—

Only God's Doing Has The Greatest Impact,
Partner With Him.

Plant Yourself Where God Put You.
Be Faithful In Public And Private.
In Due Time, God Will Cause You To
Flourish And Bear Much Fruits.

—m—

Don't Labor And Come Near Your Blessing,
If You Are Not Going To Enter The Fullness Of
Your Blessed Place. Don't Wait For God's Promise,
If You Are Not Going To Endure To The End To
Receive What He Promised.

—m—

Be Quick As A Magnet And You Will Attract
Many Blessings Speedily Unto You.

Rewards, Awards, Trophies And Blessings Are
Not Given In The Middle Of The Race, Assignments,
Schooling Or Games. They Are Given At The End.
If You Have Not Received Your Reward, That Means
You Have Not Fully Completed Your Task. Finish Your
Task Well And Wait Patiently For Your Reward.

—∞—

God Rewards People Differently
So Do Not Become Envious Or Jealous.
Just Remain Faithful And Your Rewards Will Come.

—∞—

Tap In By Faith When The Spirit Is Moving
Because That Is When The Difference Is Made.
Be Sensitive To The Move Of The Holy Spirit.
Don't Wait Until The Moving Is Over And Your
Blessings Pass Before You Decide To Believe God.
Believe God Now, You Can Get It Now.

Get Your Senses Out Of Your Way;
And Deploy Your Faith To Receive And
Enjoy The Blessings Of God, God's Way.

—⁓—

The Blessings Of God Never Comes Man's Way
So Keep Your Faith Parked In God.

—⁓—

Faith In God Makes All Things Possible.

God Is Not Going To Work It Out Your Way.
God Is Going To Work His Own Way
So Get Familiar With The Ways Of God.

The Heaven Controls The Season On The Earth.
When Heaven Says It's Your Season,
The Spirit Will Stir Things Up In Your Favor.
Ask For Big Things And Make A Great Move
When Favor Is At Work On Your Behalf.

Your Personal Response To What You Hear From God
And Obey; Dictates Your Results From God.

Everything, Everyone, And Every Situation
We Encounter In Life Begins A Journey Forward
Or Backwards Based Upon Our Response.

—⁓—

You Are Swiftly Heading To Greatness
So Don't Complain. Hold Your Head
Up And Keep Smiling.

—⁓—

Stay Focused. Do Not Allow The Distractions
From The Outside To Hi-Jack The Greatness
On Your Inside. The Inside Is Always More
Powerful Than The Outside.

Submission Is The Pathway
To Greatness.

—✺—

Submission Is Permission
For God's Provisions.

—✺—

You Must Sacrifice The Pleasure
And Comfort Of Today To Reap The Blessings
And Prosperity Of Your Future.

Your Life Is At Stake If You Do Nothing
For Your Future, And Your Future Is At Stake
If You Do Nothing With Your Life.

—∭—

The Continuation Of Your Life
Is In Your Future.

—∭—

Your Future Is Not Where You Are Going,
But Who You Are Becoming Every Day.

The Future Belongs To Faster Accurate Runners,
Not Sitters, Not Walkers, Not Talkers, Not Sleepers,
Not Slaggers, Not Stragglers Etc. No, No, No.

Your Future Existed Before Your Present,
Your Future Is God Past So Let His Spirit Lead You.

When You Dwell Solely On Your Past,
The Present Will Pass You By Erase The Very
Existence Of Your Future.

You Cannot Rewrite Your Past But You Can
Create A Very Beautiful Future. Your Past Is Like
Spilled Water In The Cultivated Soil Of Life. Just As
You Cannot Pick Up The Spilled Water So You Cannot
Change Your Past. Yesterday Is Gone. Today Is Moving
Fast To An End. Tomorrow Is Coming Quicker Than
You Have Realized. What You Don't Have Today,
You Will Have Surplus Tomorrow If You Get
A New Mindset And Do Things Different.

———

Don't Let Your History Dictate Your Destiny.

———

Great Men And Women Do Not Live
And Strive Because Of Their History.
They Do Because They Believe In An
Ongoing Multiplying Greater Destiny.

Your Mind, Mouth, Movements
Equal Your Destiny.

In Order To Succeed At Anything,
You Must Consistently Align Your Mind,
Mouth And Movements In The Same Direction.

The Soundness Of Your Mind
Is The Power Of Great Actions.

Your Mind Is The Control Center Of Your Actions.
What You Put In Your Mind Comes Out Through
Your Decisions And Actions. Whoever Or Whatever
Controls Your Mind Controls Your Life.

—⟋⟋—

Our Greatest Asset Is Our Mind. With Our Mind,
We Can Give Birth To A New Beautiful Beginning
Despite An Ugly Past. All Things Are Created Twice,
First In Our Minds And Second By Our Actions.
Therefore, We Can Create A Good, New Future By
Embracing New Thoughts And Taking New Actions.

—⟋⟋—

Keep Your Spiritual Mindsight Above Your Natural
Eyesight And Mindset Because Your Spiritual Mindsight
Can See Unlimitedly Into Your Future And Comprehend
Unseen And Seen Things Far Beyond Your Five Senses.

Sometimes You Have To Prayerfully And Wisely
Separate Or Disconnect From Things, Places And
People That Serve As A Hindrance To Your Well
Being, And Success Of Your Future.

—◊◊◊—

You May Have Started Wrong,
But You Can End Right.

—◊◊◊—

Sometimes Our Biggest Problem Is That We
Are Not Willing And Ready To Walk Away From
Our Hindrances. Therefore, We Never Experience
The Best Things, Places And People God Has In
Store For Us.

To Excel At Your Goals, You Must Focus Like
You Are Driving In The Tunnel. There Are Only
Two Things You Can Do When Driving Through
The Tunnel; That Is To Look Ahead And Keep
Driving Forward. Never Stop While Driving In The
Tunnel It Will Cause Major Delays Or Even Worst,
Major Accidents.

—ɯ—

Never Give Up Because Sometimes Our Best Results,
Come After Our Worst Experience.

—ɯ—

People Get Older And Weaker Faster Than
Their Age So Organize Your Life, Prioritize Your
Goals And Work With Creativity And Passion To
Make Your Vision Become Your Reality.

A Mental Picture Of Your Future Which Is A Vision,
Transformed Into A Physical Picture Which Can Be
In The Form Of A Written Plan, Painting On A Paper
Or Board, Diagram, Statue Image, Photo Shot, Sculpture
Structure Etc. Will Eventually Lead To The Actualization
Of Its Reality. Draw A Picture Of Your Tomorrow For
Every Aspect Of Your Life And See Yourself Being It.

—m—

Dwelling On Past Successes Or Failures
Have The Potential To Place A Stopper On Your
Accomplishment Of Greater Things Tomorrow.

—m—

What You Take For Granted,
You Will Not Have Forever,
Value What You Have And
Make The Most Of It.

No Matter What We Say Or Do,
If It Is Not On Time; It Has Less Value Or No Value.

What You Don't Care For Today,
You Will Pay For Tomorrow.
When You Ignore Warnings And Good Advice,
You Will End Up Paying Too Much For Too Little.

The Things That Are Relevant Today
Will Expire Tomorrow.

There Must Always Be Something Greater,
Big Or Small To Work Towards As Long As
You Have Life.

—〜—

Life Is A School And Everyone Is A Teacher.
They Teach You What To Be And What Not To Be.

—〜—

Live To Learn And Learn To Live Better.
Make Learning The Right Things Your Lifestyle.

What You Learn At Home As You Grow Up,
Is What You Will Use To Make Your Own Home
Tomorrow, So Don't Be Stubborn. Pay Attention,
Learn Something Worthwhile So That Your Own
Home Tomorrow Can Be Better Than Your
Parents Home Today.

When You Stop Learning, You Stop Knowing.
When You Stop Knowing, You Stop Improving
So You Become Irrelevant To Your Society.
You Become A Liability Instead Of An Asset.
Keep Learning.

Adopt These Two Things:
Jesus Christ Woke Up Every Morning With
Only One Agenda: To Please His Heavenly Father
And Give His Best To Mankind. He Only Did
Those Two Things Until His Death, Burial,
Resurrection And Ascension.

God Made Work As Part Of The Sustainer
Of Human Life. Anything That Stops Working
Is Gotten Rid Off.

—m—

Go To Work Early. Work Smarter,
Work Harder, Work Faster And Maintain
A Positive Attitude. You Will Succeed.

—m—

Work Develops Your Gifts And Skills.
Work Exposes The Ideas, Dreams, Gifts
And Skills You Have Hidden On The Inside.
Work Brings You Economic And Social
Freedom And Success.

Good Work Puts You In Demand And Make Your Gifts And Skills Marketable. Work Is A Stage To Display Your Ideas, Gifts, Talents And Skills To The Outside World. Work Will Make Your Dreams, Visions And Goals Become A Reality.

—◊—

Work Is Required To Make Or Build Anything Great. Work Enhances Creativity And Enables Good Workers To Discover The Unknown.

—◊—

It Takes Your Personal, Passionate, Intentional, Extraordinary Work To Produce Extraordinary Results.

Workers Are Builders And Builders Are Workers.
If You Will Build Any Aspect Of Your Life,
Consistent Work Is Required By You.

—⁂—

Work Is An Opportunity To Make The Invisible Visible.
That Is Why Faith Without Works Is Dead.

—⁂—

Genuine Success Has A Lot More To Do With You
Being Better, Instead Of Just Things Being Better.
God Worked Six Days To Create The Earth.
If God Could Work, How About You?
Anything That Is Not Working Is Gotten Rid Of.

The Better You Want Your Life To Become,
The More Responsibilities You Have To Accept
And The More Initiatives You Have To Take.

—⁂—

Great Results Are Products Of God's Power,
Sound Thoughts, Spirit Led Timely Movements
And Hard Work.

—⁂—

Good Results Are Never Produced Sitting,
They Are Produced By Using The Right Words,
Talking To The Right People And Doing The Right
Things At The Right Time.

You Are Responsible For The Results You Desire,
No One Else Is. Every Help You Receive Is A Favor
So Be Grateful And Appreciate It.

—⁓—

Being Responsible Means Making Wise Decisions
And Doing What Needs To Be Done, With Whom
It Needs To Be Done With, When It Needs To Be Done,
How It Needs To Be Done, Where It Needs To Be Done,
Without Being Told To Do It.

—⁓—

Sometimes, We Spent All Our Lives
Chasing Material Things, Comfort And Pleasure.
Nothing Is Wrong With Having Good Things
If You Get Them Honestly But Don't Let The
Things You Have Control You.

Your Gift Is A Solution To Somebody Else's Problem.
You Are Paid For The Problem You Solved,
On The Other Hand, You Pay For The Problem You Create.
Better To Be Paid, Than To Pay Because Sometimes,
Little Problem Have A High Price.

—᠉᠉—

Don't Let Your Job Affect You Negatively Instead,
You Affect Your Job Positively. Be A Thermostat
And Not A Thermometer. A Thermostat Sets The
Temperature For The Surrounding Atmosphere
Whereas A Thermometer Only Records The
Temperature.

—᠉᠉—

When We Focus On What We Are Good At,
We Make Room For Others To Do What They Are Best At;
Then Our Lives Become A Blessing To Others,
And Succeed With Our Gifts And Callings.

Your Appearance, Your Facial Expression,
Your Choice Of Words, Your Tone Of Voice,
Your Reaction To Situation And Your Approach
To Others, All Help To Create A Peaceful
And Productive Work Atmosphere.

Never Speak Without Authority And Authorization,
Because Words Are The Most Powerful Tool
Humans Have, And People Are Held Accountable
For What They Say.

Everything And Everyone Trusted To Your Care,
You Are Accountable For.

Every Time You Open Your Mouth,
You Are Either Speaking Life Or Death
Over Your Life And Situation.
Your Spirit-Filled Words Do Three Things;
Build Up, Teardown Or Justify.

—⚬—

Spirit-Filled Spoken Words Have Both Creative
And Destructive Supernatural Power.

—⚬—

All Things Are Formed And Done By Words.

Our Spoken Words, Form Our Living World.
Most Of What Has Occurred In Your Life Over The Years,
Are Things You Thought And Spoke Consistently.

—⁂—

Without Communication You Are Locked Up
In The Prison Of Loneliness And Isolated From
The Rest Of The World.

—⁂—

Spoken Words Are The Only Distinction
Between Human Being And Other Creatures.

Words Control And Express The Motion
And Emotions Of All Living And Non Living Beings.

—∭—

Association Leads To Classification
And Identification.

—∭—

Your Ears Are Double Windows To Your Mind
And Your Eyes Are Double Doors To Your Mind.
Some Of The Ways In Which We Can Maintain
A Sound Mind Is By Avoiding Wrong Company
And Looking Straight Ahead Or May I Say Avoiding
Attractive Distractions. Be Mindful Of What You
Allow Your Ears To Hear, And What You Allow
Your Eyes To Constantly Watch.

God Give Us Two Ears
And One Mouth Which Means You
Should Listen More And Talk Less.

—◊—

We Live To Listen And Learn;
And We Learn To Understand And Live Better.

—◊—

The Wisdom Of Silent Thoughts
Always Produces A Far Better Outcome
Than Instant Emotional Reaction.

Humility Is The Elevator To The Highest Level
Of Honor And Success Whilst Pride Is The Escalator
To The Lowest Level Of Failure And Destruction.

—◊—

Don't Let Degrees, Money, Fame, Position,
Power Or Popularity Make You Look Down
On Others Or Become A Nightmare To
Your Love Ones Instead Of A Blessing.
Stay Humble And Peaceful.

—◊—

Being Humble And Helpful To Others
Are More Important Than Exalting Oneself
Above Others.

Our Whole Purpose In Life Is Relationships
And Service Build Good Standing Relationships
With God And Others. Serve God And Others
With The Spirit Of Humility And Excellence.

—◊◊◊—

Those Who Win Never Give Up On
Doing Great Things For Others In Need.

—◊◊◊—

The Only Lasting Things We Leave With People
In This World Is Memories, Be It Good Or Bad.
You Could Have One Short Interaction With The
Person, But The Memory Could Last A Lifetime.

You Are Responsible To Leave Good Memories
Full With God's Blessings With Others.

—⁘—

Say Good And True Things About Others.
Do Good Deeds To Others And You Will
Leave Good Memories.

—⁘—

You Are Not Responsible For Others' Behavior
But You Are Responsible For Your Thoughts,
Words And Deeds To Make A Positive Difference.

Pay Close Attention To Your Personal Cheerleading Squads So That They Don't Cheer You Out Of The Will Of God Into Making Poor Decisions That Produce Disastrous Results.

———

Humans Heal Emotionally From Hugs Especially When They Are Sincere, Full Of God's Pure Love And Good Intentions From The Heart.

———

You Got To Move Faster When Someone Is Holding The Door Open For You To Enter An Opportunity Or Exit A Problem Or Else You Will Have To Open The Door For Yourself And You May Have The Keys.

Be Sensitive To Who Is Willing And Ready
To Help You Get To Your Next Level Without
Exploiting You; Connect With Them.

—m—

If Other Succeed In Making A Positive Difference,
Be A Help To Them. Do Not Be A Threat To
Their Ideas And A Hindrance To Their Efforts.

—m—

Sometimes People Ask You Many Questions,
Not Because They Want To Know Your Business,
So Don't Be Quick To Snap Them Off. They Ask
Because They Have A Strong Desire To Help You.

When You Do Not Admit To Your Existing Problems,
You Miss Out On Great Life Changing Solutions From
Others.

—⁀⁓—

Help Is Never Little When The Right Person
Receives It Because It Fulfills God's Purpose
For That Moment.

—⁀⁓—

There Is No Way Anyone Can Fulfill Their Purpose
When They Prioritize And Magnify Themselves.
Nothing Was Made For Itself. Everyone And Everything
Were Made For Service And Relationships.

Kindness Is A Bridge That Crosses Someone
Over A River Of Needs They Could Have
Drowned In.

—⟁—

Kindness Is An Irresistible Influence.
Use It Often.

—⟁—

Sometimes Letting The Wrong People In Your Life
Because Of Looks, Sweet Talk, Money And Material
Things Can Cost You Your Life At The End.

Every Best Friend Has A Best Friend That You
Don't Know. What You Think Is A Secret Is Already
Exposed To The World, It's Just A Matter Of Time.
The Things Done In Darkness Come To Light Sooner
Than Later. Anything, You Will Be Ashamed Of Publicly,
Try Not Do Them In The Dark Especially If It Is
Something That Will Ruin Your Character.

—∽—

There Are More People And Forces Who Believe
And Support You Quietly Than The Loud Voices
Who Criticize You Publicly. Keep Pressing Forward!

—∽—

If An Eagle Hangs With Ducks And Chicken
For A Long Time, It Will Begin To Think And
Act Like Them. Be Mindful Of The Mindset
Of The People You Hang With.

All Birds Have Wings, But All Birds Do Not Fly
High Because Some Birds Are Chickens And Ducks.
They Move Slowly And Pick In The Dirt. Compare
Yourself To The Eagle, You Should Aim To Fly High.
Your Potential Is Unlimited.

———

When You Discover You Are An Eagle,
You Run Away From The Chicken Coop And Pig's Pen.

———

Hang With Folks Who Are God Fearing
And Discipline. Hang With Folks Who Will
Push You Higher And Forward.

The Right Grade Of Wires Must Be Connected
In Order For The Lights To Come On, So Also
Good Relationship With The Right People Brings
Peace, Joy, Support And Fulfillment To Your Life.

———

The Company We Keep, The Books We Read,
The Faith We Exercise, The Work We Put In,
And Our Consciousness Of Timing;
Determine The Heights Of Our Destinies.

———

Good Friends Are Like Good Days.

Good Friends Are Like Sweet Gifts From
God To Give Our Lives A Good Taste;
Especially During Difficult Times.

—ɯ—

The More Good Friends We Have,
The More Good Days We Experience.

—ɯ—

Relationship With The Wrong People Always Bring
Chaos, Confusion And Stagnation In Your Life.

Not Everyone You Like, You Can Trust For Your Well Being. Some Folks Will Betray You Split Seconds For Material Things, Position Or A New Friend.

—⁓—

A Person Who Cannot Be Truthful
Should Not Be Trusted.

—⁓—

Not Everyone Can Stand To See You Accumulate Mass Wealth Because Of Your Sacrificial Private Obedience To God Without Wealth.

Some Things, Some People, Some Places,
Some Fashions And Some Habits Are Like Crazy Glue.
Easy To Attach To But Hard To Break Off From.
Be Mindful Of What And Who You Get Attached To.
They Or It Can Or Will Become A Blessing Or A Burden.
They Or It Will Push You Up Or Bring You Down.
Give You Joy Or Bring You Sorrows.

—✸—

Attachment Is A Hindrance To Progress.

—✸—

Forgiveness Settles All Matters, Not Revenge.

Forgiveness Is God's Tool To Solve And End
Problems Whereas Unforgiveness Is The Devil's
Tool To Continue And Increase The Problem.

—◊—

Unforgiveness Is A Trap That Keeps You Stuck
In An Invisible Offensive Environment.

—◊—

When You Don't Forgive, You Are Working For The Devil.
When You Forgive You Are Working For God.

You Must Be Quick To Admit When You Are Wrong And Repent So That You Can Maintain A Good Conscious. This Will Enable You To Discern Between Right And Wrong At All Times.

—∞—

Bitterness Is A Major Hindrance To A Happy And Successful Life So Be Quick To Forgive.

—∞—

God's Love Is The Key That Sets People Free Because It Is Unconditional.

I've Received God's Love, So I Live To Love,
And I Love To Live Because God Is Love.

You Don't Have To Make A Mistake Before You
Come To Your Senses. Rather, Come To Your Senses
Before You Make A Major Mistake Because Some Mistakes
Have Automatic, Lifetime, Costly Price Attached To Them.

Sometimes, You Cannot Foresee How Damaging
To The Success Of Your Life Some Mistakes Are,
Until You Have To Deal With The Consequences
On A Daily Basis.

A Little Bit, Leads To A Little More And A Little
More Leads To Addiction. Say No The First Time
And You Won't Have To Worry About The Second.
You Have The Right To Be Uncommon.

—m—

Sexual Immorality Has The Highest Promotion In The
Secular World. At The Same Time, Sexual Misconduct
Is The Fastest Way To Defame Ones Character And
Degrade Ones Standard And Status In Society.
Be Wise, Say No To Nonmarital Sex.

—m—

Lust Is Attracted To The Beauty Of The Body
But Pure Love Is Attracted To The Heart.

Dress Modestly, Covering Is Protection From External Pollution Or Danger. Everything And Every One Of High Value And Importance Is Protected By Covering. Covering Attracts Respect And Proper Approach.

—⟋⟍—

Seductive Attires Sometimes Lead To Sexual Attraction And Predators Instead Of Genuine Love.

—⟋⟍—

Don't Create Something Unnecessary To Deal With, When You Can Easily Avoid It.

Without Integrity Everything
Is A Waste Of Time.

———ᴍ———

When Our Integrity Is Compromised,
It Hijacks Our Spiritual Blessings.
We Must Be Strong Spiritually In Order
Not To Compromise Morally.

———ᴍ———

Everything Political Is Not Right And Everything Right
Is Not Political. You Rather Do What Is Right Then Be
Political Because One Day Sooner Than Later You Will
Give An Account To God.

Anything Dirty Is Always Rejected.
Dirty Hands Always Leave Behind Retraceable Print.
Dirty Deeds Only Stay Cover For A Short Time.

———✖———

Condition And Situations Are No Reasons To
Give The Devil A Place In Your Life, Your Home,
Your God Connected Relationship With Others.
You Will Regret Later. The Devil Is The Master Skillful
Deceiver. All He Wants Is For You To Begin To Open
Your Mind To His Half Truth Thoughts And Suggestions,
That Make You Feel Good And Others Look Bad In Your
Eyes. This Creates Confusion, Division, Weakness And
Defeat Mostly For You.

———✖———

What You Think Is A Problem Is Not A Problem;
You Just Need Understanding Of What You Are
Doing Wrong And Change It.

Consistent Sinful Thoughts And Acts,
Will Kill Your Future.

133

Sin Is A Killer Of Godly Destiny.

Sin Is Like Living On Death Road.

Wrong Exposure Leads To Contamination
And Destruction. Watch What You Watch.

134

—m—

When You Live A Loose Life, You Will Lose
Every Precious Thing Entrusted To Your Care.

—m—

You Can Have A Lot In Your Hands
But If You Have Nothing In Your Heart And Head,
You Will End Up Losing All That Is In Your Hands.

Your Treasures Are In Where Your Heart Is.

135

—ɰ—

You Will Find Your Treasure In Your Gift
Keep Getting Better At It.

—ɰ—

Best Results Come From Whose Minds And Hands
Your Problems Are Left In.

The Success And Prosperity Of Our Lives
Are In YOUR MINDSET AND ATTITUDE;
It Is Not Dependent On Nothing And No One Else.

———

Your Mindset And Attitude Are The Two
Most Important Things Every Human Being
Should Improve Every Day.

———

Until You Improve Your Mindset,
You Cannot Improve Your Life.

Your Mindset About Your Challenges
Determine Your Overwhelming Victory
Or Defeat At The End So Think Positive.

—m—

Restraining Your Mind To Think Right
And Stay Focused Is Mandatory For Success
In Every Aspect Of Your Life And Ministry.

—m—

Both God, Life, And Situations Respect,
Responds And Rewards Only Your
Mindset And Attitudes.

The Thoughts Of Your Mind, The Extreme Passion
Of Your Desire, The Belief Of Your Heart,
The Works Of Your Hands Will Destroy Your
Excuses And Make Your Dream Your Reality.

—w—

Control Your Life, By Controlling Your Thoughts
Because Your Mind Is A Magnet To What You
Consistently Think About.

—w—

What You Believe Will Control Your Behavior
In All Circumstances And Situation.

How Far And How High We See Ourselves
Determine How High We Ascend, How Wide
We Expand And How Far We Extend.

—⟋⟍—

Nothing Is As Strong As A Made Up Mind.

—⟋⟍—

Everything You Say And Do Is A Seed You Are Sowing.
Never Forget, The Seeds You Sow, Only Bear Fruits
In Your Life.

Take Nothing And No One For Granted.
Everything And Every Moment Is An Opportunity
Because Everything And Every Moment Is Temporary.
Therefore, Understand The Purpose Of The Opportunity
And Make The Most Of It With A Sense Of Urgency
Because It Is Only For A Moment.

—☙—

Opportunities Are Birthed In Your Spirit,
Seen With The Mind Of Your Understanding
And Materialize By Your Decision And Actions.

—☙—

When You Do Not See The Opportunity In Situations,
Places And Divine Connection With Certain People,
Or Understand The Purpose Of The Opportunity To
Fulfill It To Its Fullest, You Will Miss Out On Your Next
Opportunity Because Your Blessing And Direction To Your
Next Opportunity Is Hidden In The Opportunity You
Have Right Now. Pray For Spiritual Enlightenment.

Every Opportunity Is To Prepare You
And Lead You To Your Next Opportunity.

—m—

The Rain Suppose To Rain And The Sun Suppose
To Shine. The Whole World Will Suffer If The Sun
Chooses To Stop Shining, And Be Like The Rain.
Never Forget, The Sun Always Shines Through The Rain.
You Are Like The Sun So Keep Shinning Despite The
Challenges And Negative Attitude Of Others.

—m—

God Does Not Process People To Be Like
Somebody Else. God Processes People So That
They Can Be Prepared To Fulfill Their God Given
Purpose And Become Better Than Their Best.

Don't Cut Your Process Of Preparation Short
Or Else You Will Never Become Your Best And
Fulfill Your Purpose To The Fullest.
Stay In Your Training Process To The End.

—◆—

Proper Preparation Is A Process That Is Necessary
To Produce Excellent Results.

—◆—

Anyone You See Fulfilling Their Purpose, Has Been
Through Some Form Rigorous Preparation Process.
Don't Envy Others, Go Through Your Process And
Stay There Until God Says Your Faith Is Strong Enough
And Your Character Is Solid And Stable Enough To
Handle The Test Of Your Next Level His Way.

Plan Ahead And Prepare To Make
Your Plan A Successfully Reality.
Writing Your Vision On Paper Prepares
You For Timely Right Actions.

—◊—

Dreams And Visions Remain ONLY Dreams And Visions
In Our Hearts And Head; Until They Are WRITTEN On
Paper In A Simple Laser Clear Format With PURPOSE,
DATES, PLACE, AND TIME That Anyone Can Read,
Understand And Followed With Daily Accountable,
Relentless, Committed, Consistent, Timely ACTIONS
To Produce Desired Results.

—◊—

God Is A Prepared God And He Deals
With Prepared People. Expectation Without
Preparation Equals Embarrassment.

Prepare For What You Expect Or Else Your
Expectation Will Become An Embarrassment When
It Shows Up Instead Of A Blessing. It Is Better And
Wiser To Be Prepared Before Moving From One
Stage Of Life To The Other.

—◊—

The Man Who Is Unprepared
Never Gets The Job Done Effectively.

—◊—

Slow Down Before You Take Off And Ensure
That You Have What You Need For Your Journey.
So, When You Finally Take Off, You Won't Have
To Slow Down.

Your Strength Or Gift Should Be
Mastered Privately, Displayed Publicly
Only For The Fulfillment Of Purpose.

—⚬—

Your Strength Is Your Sacred Weapon
To Ensure Your Victory.

—⚬—

Let Your Private Life Drive Your Public Life
So That You Don't Have Many Shameful
And Hurtful Accidents Publicly. .

Being Careful Is More Important Than Being Able.
If You Are Not Careful In Handling A Situation,
Thing Or Person, You Can Ruin Something Beautiful
In The Process Or Even Make A Situation Worse
Than It Was.

—⟋⟍—

By God's Grace, You Can Do Without What You Think
You Cannot Do Without. Pray, Focus, Figure Out A Way,
Discipline Yourself And Get The Job With Excellence.

—⟋⟍—

You Can Miss God's Presence And Purpose,
Being Protected By Prayerless People.

Being Prayerful Before Making Decisions
Is Wiser And More Beneficial Than Being
Knowledgeable And Hasty.

—⁂—

You Are Creature Of All Possibilities
So Remove Yourself From All Limitations
By Praying For Awareness, Wisdom, Direction,
Craving Self-Discipline, And The Power To Do
Relentless Creative Work.

—⁂—

Believe Is The Mother Of All Possibilities,
And The Power Of Your Abilities.

When You Believe, You Don't Complain Instead,
You Pray, And Work Relentlessly Towards What
You Believe Until It Becomes Your Reality.

—⟋⟍—

Wake Up Spiritually, Wake Up And Pray.
As A Believer, You Must Battle Spiritually Against
The Forces Of Darkness In Prayer At Midnight,
When The Old Day Dies And The New Day
Is Birthed So That You Can Experience Victory,
Success And Dominion During The New Day.

—⟋⟍—

Anyone Who Thinks That He Or She Can Fight
A Spiritual Or Physical Battle While He Or She Sleeps,
Will Be Beaten Well By Their Enemy Easily.
Wake Up! Fast And Pray For Your Personal Breakthrough.

Strategies To Win, Are More Effective
Than Strength; So Pray For Winning Strategies.

———*———

You Leave Yourself Stuck Under Spiritual Blindness,
Strong Fleshly Influence And Spiritually Powerless
When You Choose Not To Fast And Pray Periodically
Throughout The Year.

———*———

You Don't Hear Truth In The Crowd.
Instead The Truth Comes Out In One On One
Fellowship; When You Hang Around After The
Crowd Leaves. Learn To Hang Around In God's
Presence After Prayer.

Low Things Are Controlled From High Places.
Every Problem Below Has A Remote Control
Above In Consistent Prayers.

—m—

Even Though You Have A Set Of Natural Eyes,
You Still Need Light To See. Without The Sun Light
The World Will Be Dark Outside. Without The Electric
Light, The Inside Of Houses, Buildings And Streets Will
Be Dark Also. Bottom Line Is, Even With 20/20 Vision,
Without Light You Cannot See. Spiritually, God's Word
Is A Lamp To Your Feet To Your Feet And A Light
To Your Path.

—m—

Physical Medicine Can Only Heal
The Body Sometimes, But Prayers Can Heal
The Spirit, Soul And Body All The Times.

It Is A Terrible Thing To Reject And Devalue
What God Has Given You To Bless Your Life
Because It Is Not Dress Up Or Located According
To Your Description.

—ᴍ—

People Do Not Respect And Value
What They Don't Deserve So Don't Give It To Them.

—ᴍ—

Sometimes Your Life Is Far Better Off
With The Little You Have Than The People
You See And Admire With The Fame,
Fortune And Hidden Misery.

Gratitude Is Always The Most Appreciated Attitude,
So Be Grateful.

—m—

Receiving Is The Result Of Giving First In Most Cases.
Don't Worry About Receiving Just Continue To Give
Service And Gifts To Others.

—m—

Receiving Is Limitation And But Giving Is Multiplication.
All Humans Were Created Out Of Giving.
All Positive Differences Are Made By Sacrificial Giving.

Receiving Without Giving Produces Suffocation.
Always Give More Than You Receive,
And You Will Always Have To Give More.

—⁂—

You Cannot Succeed, If You Always
Want To Receive And Never Give.

—⁂—

Always Wanting To Receive But Never Giving Back
Is Bad Practice. Hands That Are Not Useful To Its
Own Body And Serviceable To Others Are Bad Hands.

Your Life Is Like A Beautiful Flower Garden.
Keep It Trimmed With Self-Discipline,
Watered With Prayers, Fertilized With Love
And Decorated With Real Good Friends.

—⁓—

Beauty Is Always Seen Where Things
Are Clean And In Order.

—⁓—

The Beauty Of Every Miracle
Is The Time That It Happens.